Grammar
PRACTICE BOOK

Mc Graw Hill **Macmillan/McGraw-Hill**

A

The *McGraw·Hill* Companies

 Macmillan/McGraw-Hill

Published by Macmillan/McGraw-Hill, of McGraw-Hill Education, a division of The McGraw-Hill Companies, Inc.,
Two Penn Plaza, New York, New York 10121.

Printed in the United States of America

3 4 5 6 7 8 9 10 WDQ 13 12 11 10

Contents

Unit 1 • Friends and Family

Unit 2 • Community Heroes

Unit 3 • Let's Create

Unit 4 • Better Together

Unit 5 • Growing and Changing

Unit 6 • The World Around Us

Name _____

- A **sentence** is a group of words that tells a complete thought.
- Every sentence begins with a capital letter.
- A **statement** is a sentence that tells something. It ends with a period.

  School is fun.   We play in the gym.

Circle each sentence. Then complete each incomplete sentence. Write it on the lines below.

1. Our classroom is sunny.
2. Writes on the chalkboard.
3. We read books.
4. Like art class.
5. Recess is a fun part of the day.

art c

_____

_____

_____

_____

- A **question** is a sentence that asks something. It ends with a question mark.
- A **statement** is a sentence that tells something. It ends with a period.
- Begin each statement and question with a capital letter.

  Do you have a pencil?   I have paper.

Read the sentences. Circle each question, and underline each statement.

1. Do you have homework?

2. I have lots of homework.

3. What do you have to do?

4. I have to read a story.

5. The story is about a pig.

6. Does Frank have homework?

7. Frank has to write a story.

8. What kind of story will he write?

9. Will he write a funny story?

10. No, he will write a scary one.

© Macmillan/McGraw-Hill

- Begin each sentence with a capital letter.
- End a statement with a period.
- End a question with a question mark.

    We have gym today.
    What is in my backpack?

Read the sentences. Write the sentences correctly on the lines.

1. what do you bring to school

   _____

2. i bring books and a pencil

   _____

3. what else is in your backpack

   _____

4. my lunch is in my backpack

   _____

5. what did you bring for lunch

   _____

6. do you want to sit with me at lunch time

   _____

7. my new teacher is nice

   _____

8. Are we in the same class

   _____

- A sentence tells a complete thought.
- Begin each sentence with a capital letter.
- End a statement with a period.
- End a question with a question mark.

Read the passage. Circle each mistake in capitalization and punctuation. Then rewrite the passage correctly on the lines below.

Today is Monday What do we do first. the teacher Reads a story. then we have math. does each child have a pencil. Now we are ready to begin the lesson

_____

_____

_____

_____

Name _____

Add the correct end mark to each sentence.
Write S next to each statement.
Write Q next to each question.

1. Our new school opens today _____

2. The brick building has three floors _____

3. Where is your classroom _____

4. The playground has three swing sets _____

5. How tall is the shiny new slide _____

6. Did you see the new music room _____

7. There is a band concert tonight _____

8. My sister plays in the school band _____

9. What instrument does she play _____

10. Do you have tickets to the concert _____

Name _____

> • A **command** is a sentence that tells someone to do something. It ends with a period.
>
>   Share with your friends.   Listen to your mother.

Circle each command.

1. I like to play games.

2. Treat the animals with care.

3. Sing a song with me.

4. Where does your friend live?

5. Share your cookie.

6. My dogs are my best friends.

7. I am going to Laura's birthday party next week.

8. Sit next to me.

9. Who gave you that flower?

10. Take me to the park.

Write two new commands on the lines.

_____

_____

_____

_____

© Macmillan/McGraw-Hill

Name _____

- An **exclamation** is a sentence that shows strong feelings. It ends with an exclamation point.
- Begin each exclamation with a capital letter.

   We love the zoo!
   Wow, those are huge elephants!

A. Underline each exclamation.

1. Today is Saturday.

2. Hooray, we are going to the zoo!

3. We will see many animals.

4. That giraffe is gigantic!

5. The lions look hungry.

6. Oh no, I'm scared!

7. The seals are so cute!

8. What time do you feed the seals?

9. The zoo closes in one hour.

10. We had so much fun!

B. Write two new exclamations on the lines.

_____

_____

Name _____

- Begin each sentence with a capital letter.
- End each command with a period.
- End an exclamation with an exclamation point.

  Help your friend.   This homework is hard!

**Read the sentences. Write the
sentences correctly on the lines.**

1. please come to my birthday party.

_____

2. this is an awesome party

_____

3. cut the cake now

_____

4. i'm stuffed

_____

5. turn the music down

_____

6. play cards with me

_____

7. this is fun

_____

8. please help me clean up

_____

- Begin each sentence with a capital letter.
- End a **command** with a period and an **exclamation** with an exclamation point.

Circle each capitalization and punctuation mistake. Then rewrite the passage correctly on the lines.

let's go to our baseball game. you are up to bat first Watch out, here comes the ball. hit it hard. hooray, it's a home run.

_____

_____

_____

_____

© Macmillan/McGraw-Hill

Name _____

Add a period to each command.
Add an exclamation point to each exclamation.

1. Hooray, the sun is shining brightly ____

2. Come and play in my yard ____

3. Look at our new puppy ____

4. Gosh, your puppy is so little ____

5. Roll over ____

6. Oh no, the puppy rolled in the mud ____

Add or take away words to rewrite the sentences.

7. Make this statement a command.

   Jake scratches the puppy's belly.

   _____

8. Make this statement an exclamation.

   Your puppy is cute.

   _____

© Macmillan/McGraw-Hill

Name _____

> • Every sentence has two parts.
>
> • The **subject** tells who or what does something.
>
>   <u>Firefighters</u> put out a fire.   <u>Dogs</u> like to run.
>   subject   subject

A. Underline the subject in each sentence.

1. The man calls the fire station.

2. The family leaves the house.

3. Everyone looks at the flames.

4. A fire truck races to the house.

5. The firefighters are just in time.

B. Write another sentence about a fire. Circle the subject.

6. _____

_____

Name _____

> • You can correct some incomplete sentences by adding a subject.
>
> • A **subject** tells who or what does something.
>
> Incomplete sentence: live at the firehouse
>
> Complete sentence with a subject: The firefighters live at the firehouse.

Add a subject to the incomplete sentences and rewrite them on the lines below.

1. Visited the firehouse.

_____

2. Climbed inside a red fire truck.

_____

3. Taught us about fire safety.

_____

4. Told us to never play with matches.

_____

5. Told us to write about fire safety for homework.

_____

_____

© Macmillan/McGraw-Hill

- Begin the greeting and closing in a letter with a capital letter.
- Use a comma after the greeting in a letter.
- Use a comma after the closing in a letter.

> Dear Mom,
>
> Love,
>
> Kim

Rewrite the letter correctly.

dear Grandma and Grandpa

I am having a great time on vacation. I miss you.

love

Juan

_____

_____

_____

_____

Name _____

- Begin the greeting and closing of a letter with a capital letter.
- Use commas after the greeting and closing in a letter.

Rewrite the letter correctly on the lines below.

dear Mom and Dad

am having a great time at camp. sing around the campfire. takes good care of us. can't wait for visiting day!

love

Maria

_____

_____

_____

_____

Name _____

Write C next to each complete sentence and circle the subject. Write I next to each incomplete sentence. Then add a subject and rewrite the sentences on the lines below. Underline the subject.

1. Our family has a fire escape plan. _____

2. My mom drew a map of our house. _____

3. shows the way out of the house. _____

4. practiced the escape plan many times. _____

5. Our meeting place is on the corner of our street. _____

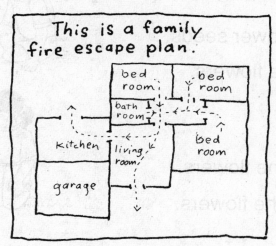

_____

_____

_____

Name _____

- There are two parts to every sentence.
- The **subject** tells who or what the sentence is about.
- A **predicate** tells what the subject does or is.

Jane <u>plants flowers</u>.
predicate

Which sentence tells about the picture?
Draw a line under the predicate of
that sentence.

1. **a.** Jane plants flower seeds.

   b. Jane picks the flowers.

2. **a.** Jane smells the flowers.

   b. Jane waters the flowers.

3. **a.** The flowers are pink and yellow.

   b. The sun shines on the flowers.

4. **a.** The flowers are dying now.

   b. Jane picks the flowers now.

Name _____

> • A **predicate** tells what the subject of a sentence does or is.
>
> • You can correct some incomplete sentences by adding a predicate.
>
>   Incomplete sentence: My dad
>
>   Complete sentence: My dad loves vanilla ice cream.

Draw lines to match each subject with a predicate to make a complete sentence. Then write the sentences on the lines below.

1. An ice-cream truck   dropped his cone.

2. The driver   ate her cone quickly.

3. Mia   drove into the park.

4. Sam   sold ice cream.

1. _____

2. _____

3. _____

4. _____

Name _____

- Use a comma between the day and year in a date.
- Use a comma between the names of a city and a state.

August 17, 2006   Denver, Colorado

Read the sentences. Make the corrections. Write the correct sentences on the lines.

1. Abby was born on February 6 1998.

_____

2. She was born in Brooklyn New York.

_____

3. Her family moved to Portland Oregon.

_____

4. They moved on October 14 2003.

_____

Name _____

- Use a comma between the day and year in a date.
- Use a comma between the names of a city and a state.

Draw a line below each mistake in the letter. Then rewrite the letter correctly on the lines.

Dear Uncle Ted,

I can't wait to visit you in Los Angeles California! We are coming on December 23 2007. I'll be sad when we leave there on January 2 2008.

It is so cold here in Burlington Vermont! The snow.

Love,

Noah

_____

_____

_____

_____

_____

Name _____

Fill in the circle next to the predicate of the sentence.

I. My sister Rosa made a clay boat.

○ My sister Rosa

○ a clay boat

○ made a clay boat

2. She entered the boat in an art contest.

○ She entered

○ entered the boat in an art contest

○ boat in an art contest

3. The boat won first prize.

○ won first prize

○ The boat

○ first prize

4. Rosa is taking art classes now.

○ Rosa is

○ art classes

○ is taking art classes now

5. Her teacher called her a true artist.

○ called her a true artist

○ a true artist

○ Her teacher

- If two sentences have the same predicate, you can combine them to make one sentence.
- You can combine sentences by joining two subjects with **and**.

<u>Ana</u> learned English.   <u>Pedro</u> learned English.

<u>Ana and Pedro</u> learned English.

Combine the subjects in each pair of sentences to make one sentence. Write the new sentence on the lines.

1. Ana moved here from Chile.

   Pedro moved here from Chile.

   _____

2. Our teacher welcomed Ana.

   The principal welcomed Ana.

   _____

3. Josh played soccer with Pedro.

   Hope played soccer with Pedro.

   _____

4. Ana made friends.

   Pedro made friends.

   _____

- If two sentences have subjects that are the same, you can combine the sentences.
- You can combine sentences by joining the predicates with **and**.

  Aki was born in Japan.   Aki lives in America.

  Aki was born in Japan and lives in America.

Combine the predicates in each pair of sentences to make one sentence. Write the new sentence on the line.

1. Aki speaks Japanese.   Aki writes in English.

_____

2. Aki has brown hair.   Aki is tall.

_____

3. Emily sat next to Aki.   Emily shared her snack.

_____

4. Aki plays basketball.   Aki jumps rope.

_____

© Macmillan/McGraw-Hill

- Use **quotation marks** at the beginning and end of what a person says.

- A quotation shows the exact words of what a person says.

    "I like America," said Tamar.

Read each sentence. Correct the punctuation and write the corrected sentence on the lines.

1. This is Tamar, said our teacher.

   _____

2. I moved here from Israel, Tamar said.

   _____

3. Welcome to our school, Liz said.

   _____

4. Thank you, said Tamar.

   _____

5. The teacher asked, What kind of books do you like to read?

   _____

   _____

6. Tamar answered, I love to read books about dinosaurs.

   _____

   _____

Name _____

- Sometimes you can combine sentences by joining two subjects or two predicates with **and**.

- Use quotation marks at the beginning and end of what a person says.

Write the passage correctly on the lines. Add quotation marks where they are needed. Combine sentences that have the same subjects or predicates.

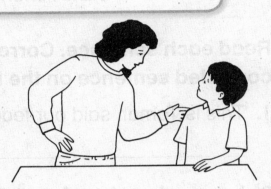

Miguel moved to Austin, Texas. His family moved to Austin, Texas. He starts his new school soon. He starts his new soccer team soon. Miguel is worried.

I miss my friends, Miguel said.

You will make new friends, said his mom.

_____

_____

_____

_____

_____

Name _____

Combine the subjects or the predicates in each pair of sentences to make new sentences. Write the new sentences on the lines.

1. Nejal lived in Turkey.

   Her family lived in Turkey.

   _____

2. Her father got a job in Virginia.

   Her father moved the family here.

   _____

3. Nejal studied hard.

   Nejal learned English quickly.

   _____

4. I met Nejal first.

   I introduced her to all the kids.

   _____

   _____

5. She smiled at everyone.

   She made friends easily.

   _____

   _____

Name _____

- A **noun** is a word that names a person, place, or thing.

- Some nouns name **people**.

  A <u>girl</u> mows the lawn.   Her <u>dad</u> plants a tree.

Circle the noun in each sentence that names a person.

1. Mom grows a vegetable garden.

2. Dad picks the vegetables.

3. My brothers eat the snap peas.

4. My sister likes the tomatoes.

Write two more sentences on the lines below. Include a noun that names a person in each one. Use the picture for ideas.

5. _____

_____

6. _____

_____

Name _____

- A noun is a word that names a person, place, or thing.
- Some nouns name **places**.

    This is my backyard.

- Some nouns name **things**.

    The flowers are yellow.

A. Read the sentences. Underline the nouns that name things. Circle the nouns that name places.

1. Many plants grow in the forest.

2. We saw evergreens in the mountains.

3. You can see a cactus in the desert.

4. What trees grow in your town?

B. Write two more sentences on the lines below. In one sentence, include a noun that names a place. In the other sentence, include a noun that names a thing.

5. _____

   _____

6. _____

   _____

- Use commas to separate three or more words in a series.
- The word **and** or **or** comes before the last word in a series.

I see flowers, plants, <u>and</u> trees.

A rose may be yellow, white, red, <u>or</u> pink.

Read each sentence. Write the corrected sentence on the line.

1. I need to buy pots soil and seeds.

_____

2. Do you want to plant tulips daisies or roses?

_____

3. Flowers need sun air and water to grow.

_____

4. Will you plant flowers in the front back or side yard?

_____

5. I will give flowers to my sister my aunt and my mom.

_____

Write another sentence about plants. Include three or more words in a series.

6. _____

_____

- A noun is a word that names a person, place, or thing.
- Use commas to separate three or more words in a series.

A. Read the passage. Add any missing commas.

Cara Max and Jack hiked up a mountain. They saw trees insects and flowers along the path. For lunch they each had a sandwich a yogurt and a drink. At the end of the hike, Max said, "I'm tired!"

B. Go back and underline each noun in the passage. Write all the nouns on the lines below.

_____   _____   _____

_____   _____   _____

_____   _____   _____

_____   _____   _____

_____   _____

Name _____

Circle the nouns in each sentence.

1. My uncle opened a shop in the city.

2. People can buy fresh fruit and vegetables there.

3. My aunt grew those berries in her garden.

4. Farmers grow other foods in their fields.

5. A huge truck brings some corn.

Write the nouns that you circled in the correct column.

People	Places	Things
_____	_____	_____
_____	_____	_____
_____	_____	_____
		_____
		_____

> • A **singular noun** names one person, place, or thing.
>
> • A **plural noun** names more than one person, place, or thing.
>
> • Add **-s** to form the plural of most nouns.
>
>   I have one <u>dog</u>.   Mia has two <u>dogs</u>.

Use the pictures to fill in each blank with a plural noun.

1. The bird is eating two _____.

2. Three _____ are sleeping.

3. The _____ are feeding the fish.

4. There are five _____ in the nest.

- Add **-es** to form the plural of singular nouns that end in **s**, **sh**, **ch**, or **x**.

  fox ⟶ foxes   lunch ⟶ lunches

- To form the plural of nouns ending in a consonant and **y**, change **y** to **i** and add **-es**.

  pony ⟶ ponies

- Some nouns change their spelling to name more than one.

  mouse ⟶ mice   man ⟶ men

Read the sentences. Make the underlined nouns plural.
Write them on the lines.

1. The <u>child</u> took a trip to the farm. _____

2. How many <u>bus</u> did they fill up? _____

3. The <u>pony</u> were eating grass. _____

4. Several <u>mouse</u> were in the barn. _____

5. For five <u>penny</u> they could feed the animals. _____

Name _____

- Begin the greeting and closing of a letter with a capital letter.
- Use a comma after the greeting in a letter.
- Use a comma after the closing in a letter.

Write the letter on the lines. Use capital letters and commas where they belong.

dear Aunt Yoon

　　Sam and I went to a fair today. Many other children were there. We rode on ponies. We had fun! We miss you.

　　　　　　love
　　　　　　Jing

_____

_____

_____

_____

- Check the spelling of all plural nouns. Add **-es** to nouns that end in **s**, **sh**, **ch**, or **x**.

- When you write a letter, check that the greeting and the closing begin with capital letters.

- Use commas after the greeting and closing in the letter.

Find each mistake in the spelling of plural nouns, capitalization, and commas. Then rewrite the letter correctly on the lines below.

dear Ms. Green

   Thank you for reading your storys to our class. We really liked the one about the three fox who live in three box. The story about the ponys who turned into mouses was great!

                    yours truly

                    Mr. Troy's class

_____

_____

_____

_____

Name _____

Complete each sentence with the nouns in ( ).
Write the nouns in their plural form.

I. The tiny _____ needed help. (bird)

2. Their _____ had fallen from the _____.
(nest, branch)

3. The _____ worked together to help. (child)

4. The _____ picked up some small _____.
(girl, twig)

5. The _____ added _____ of cloth. (boy,
scrap)

6. The baby _____ were hungry. (fox)

7. They ate _____ from the _____.
(berry, bush)

8. Some _____ came to eat the _____.
(mouse, seed)

- Some nouns name special persons, places, or things.

- This kind of noun is called a **proper noun**.

- A proper noun begins with a capital letter.

  <u>Carlos</u> was born at <u>Oakwood Hospital</u>.

Circle the proper nouns.

1. Carlos lives in New Jersey.

2. He goes to Orchard School on King Street.

3. His teacher is Mr. Fleming.

4. At recess he plays tag with Al and Sara.

5. After school the friends play at Miller Park on Oak Street.

6. On rainy days, they play Monopoly.

7. Sometimes they go to Reed Library near Reed River.

8. They like to look at the pictures in Science World Encyclopedia.

Name _____

> • Some **proper nouns** name days of the week, months, and holidays.
>
> • The name of each day, month, or holiday begins with a capital letter.
>
> <u>S</u>unday   <u>J</u>une   <u>F</u>ather's <u>D</u>ay

Choose the proper noun that names a day, month, or holiday. Write it correctly on the line below.

1. january
   winter
   vacation

   _____

2. flag
   vote
   president's day

   _____

3. holiday
   flowers
   mother's day

   _____

4. sunday
   day
   afternoon

   _____

5. fireworks
   summer
   july

   _____

6. vacation
   labor day
   weekend

   _____

7. september
   school
   teacher

   _____

8. thanksgiving
   fall
   family

   _____

Name _____

- An **abbreviation** is a short form of a word.
- An abbreviation begins with a capital letter and ends with a period.
- Most titles of people are abbreviations.

<u>Mrs.</u>   <u>Ms.</u>   <u>Mr.</u>   <u>Dr.</u>

Find the mistakes. Write each sentence correctly on the line.

1. mr Jones broke his arm.

_____

2. mrs Jones drove mr Jones to the hospital.

_____

3. dr Jimenez took an x-ray of his arm.

_____

4. ms Rose, the nurse, helped the doctor.

_____

- The names of special people, places, or things begin with capital letters. The names of days of the week, months, and holidays begin with capital letters.

- An abbreviation begins with a capital letter and ends with a period.

- The greeting and the closing of a letter begin with capital letters. Use commas after the greeting and closing in the letter.

Find each mistake in capitalization and punctuation. Rewrite the letter correctly on the lines below.

dear dr moss

Thank you for seeing me on thursday. It was very nice of you to come to elwood hospital on thanksgiving. I hope you were still able to have a nice Holiday dinner.

yours truly

lisa

_____

_____

_____

_____

_____

Circle the underlined words that are proper nouns.

1. Last <u>Monday</u>, our <u>class</u> went on a field <u>trip</u>.

2. <u>Mr. Jones</u> was our <u>driver</u>.

3. He drove from our <u>school</u> to <u>Merrit Hospital</u>.

4. <u>Westside School</u> is ten <u>miles</u> from the <u>hospital</u>.

5. The <u>bus</u> went through the <u>Third Street Tunnel</u>.

6. We met <u>Maria Cortez</u> and other <u>nurses</u> and <u>doctors</u>.

7. It was the <u>month</u> of <u>February</u>.

8. <u>Valentine's Day</u> was in two <u>days</u>.

9. Our <u>teacher</u> <u>Ms. Adams</u> had asked us to make <u>cards</u>
   for the sick children.

10. I gave my card to a <u>girl</u> named <u>Josie</u>.

Name _____

> • A **possessive noun** shows who or what owns or has something.
>
> • Add an **apostrophe** (') and **-s** to a singular noun to make it possessive.
>
>   The <u>dog's</u> bowl is empty.

Choose the correct possessive noun. Write it on the line.

1. The _____ eyes are black.
   A. rabbit
   B. rabbit's

2. The _____ babies are called ducklings.
   A. ducks
   B. duck's

3. _____ kitten is orange.
   A. Maya's
   B. Maya

4. The _____ tail wags fast.
   A. puppy
   B. puppy's

5. The snake is _____ pet.
   A. Petes
   B. Pete's

Name _____

> - Add an apostrophe to most plural nouns to make them possessive.
>
>   The <u>animals'</u> barn is red.
>
> - Add an apostrophe (') and **-s** to plural nouns that do not end in **s**.
>
>   The <u>children's</u> trip to the farm was fun.

**Underline the correct plural possessive noun in ().
Rewrite the sentence on the line below.**

1. I found several (birds'/bird's) nests in our yard.

   _____

2. The (squirrel's/squirrels') tails are bushy.

   _____

3. The (bear's/bears') bodies are very big.

   _____

4. The (mice's/mices') noses twitch when they smell a cat.

   _____

5. The (dog's/dogs') owners are training their pets.

   _____

6. The (geeses'/geese's) beaks are wet.

   _____

- Always use an apostrophe to form a possessive.
- Add an apostrophe and **-s** to make a singular noun possessive.
- Add an apostrophe to make most plural nouns possessive.

Look at the picture. Then write the possessive of each noun on the line.

1. That _____ leash is on.

2. This _____ tail is curly.

3. The _____ bowls are on the floor.

4. The _____ bowl is on the table.

Name _____

- Add an apostrophe and **-s** to make a singular noun possessive.
- Add an apostrophe to make most plural nouns possessive.

Circle each mistake. Rewrite the passage correctly on the lines below.

A frogs eggs are called egg spawn. The eggs shells protect the egg spawn. Soon the eggs hatch. Tadpoles come out. The new tadpoles tails are very long. Did you know that tadpoles eat frogs eggs?

_____

_____

_____

_____

_____

_____

Name _____

Mark the sentence that is rewritten correctly.

Underline the possessive noun in the correct sentence.

1. The wings of the butterfly are blue and black.

   ○ The butterfly's wings are blue and black.

   ○ The butterflies wings are blue and black.

   ○ The butterflys' wings are blue and black.

2. The shells of the crabs are too small now.

   ○ The crab's shells are too small now.

   ○ The crabs shells are too small now.

   ○ The crabs' shells are too small now.

3. The eggs of our duck are ready to hatch.

   ○ Our ducks eggs are ready to hatch.

   ○ Our duck's eggs are ready to hatch.

   ○ Our ducks' eggs are ready to hatch.

4. The ears of the puppy are long and floppy.

   ○ The puppies ears are long and floppy.

   ○ The puppy's ears are long and floppy.

   ○ The puppys' ears are long and floppy

5. The feathers of the swans have turned white.

   ○ The swans' feathers have turned white.

   ○ The swan's feathers have turned white.

   ○ The swans feathers have turned white.

- A **plural noun** names more than one person, place, or thing.
- To change a singular noun to a plural noun, add **-s** or **-es**. Do not add an apostrophe.

  pool ——→ pools   box ——→ boxes

Make the noun in ( ) plural. Then write the correct sentence on the line below.

1. The (player) are getting ready for the big game.

_____

2. Each team has ten (child).

_____

3. How many (coach) are there?

_____

4. Ben threw four (pitch).

_____

5. Our team scored five (run).

_____

Name _____

- Add apostrophe (') and **-s** to a singular noun to make it possessive.

    The <u>girl's</u> towel is wet.

- Add an apostrophe to make most plural nouns possessive.

    Several <u>swimmers'</u> caps are white.

Circle the mistake in each sentence. Then write the possessive noun correctly on the line below.

1. The girls goggles are on their faces.

_____

2. The boys suit is red.

_____

3. The coachs whistle is around her neck.

_____

4. All three swimmers strokes are very strong.

_____

5. The fans applause is loud.

_____

Name _____

- Add an apostrophe and **-s** to make a singular noun possessive.
- Add an apostrophe to make most plural nouns possessive.
- Do not add an apostrophe to form a plural noun.

**Underline the mistakes. Write
the sentences correctly
on the lines below.**

1. Juans check-up is today.

_____

2. There are three doctor's at the office.

_____

3. Dr. Brown is a childrens doctor.

_____

4. The doctor listens to the boys' heart.

_____

5. Juan steps on Dr. Browns' scale to be weighed.

_____

6. Nurse Ann uses a chart to check Juan's eye's.

_____

Name _____

- Add an apostrophe and **-s** to make a singular noun possessive.
- Add an apostrophe to make most plural nouns possessive.
- Do not add an apostrophe to form a plural noun.
- Use commas to separate three or more words in a series.

Find each mistake with plurals, possessives, and commas. Rewrite the passage correctly on the lines below.

At Ellas school, students choices for sports are tennis soccer and basketball. Ellas' mom and dad think she should play soccer. Her brothers favorite sport is basketball. Ella loves all sport's!

_____

_____

_____

_____

Circle the correct form of the noun to complete each sentence.

I. My coach showed us some special _____.

stretch   stretches   stretchs

2. "Do these before all your _____," she said.

practices   practice   practices'

3. Early in the year, we practiced in the _____ gym.

schools   schools'   school's

4. Later in the spring, we used one of two soccer _____.

fields'   fields   field's

5. My two best _____ moms are coaching this year.

friends'   friends   friend's

6. They like to run _____ with us.

lap's   lappes   laps

7. My _____ first game was a loss.

teams   teams'   team's

8. Both _____ words after the game made us feel better.

coaches'   coach's   coaches

Name _____

- An **action verb** is a word that shows action.
- An action verb shows what someone or something is doing.

Isabel <u>tells</u> a story.   Martin <u>listens</u> to Isabel.

Circle the action verb in each sentence. Write it on the line.

1. Justin sits in a chair. _____

2. He reads a story to his sister, Lucy. _____

3. Lucy listens to Justin. _____

4. She laughs at the funny parts. _____

5. Justin turns the pages. _____

6. He points to the pictures. _____

Write an action verb on the line to complete each sentence below. Use the picture to help you.

7. Justin _____ at his sister.

8. Lucy _____ Justin.

Name _____

- Some action verbs show actions you can see.

  Habib <u>reads</u> a book.

- Some action verbs tell about actions that are hard to see.

  Habib <u>enjoys</u> books about animals.

Read each sentence. Underline the action verb. Then write another sentence using that same verb.

I. The three bears walk in the woods.

_____

2. Goldilocks likes the porridge.

_____

3. Goldilocks sits in Baby Bear's chair.

_____

4. She breaks the chair.

_____

5. Goldilocks feels tired.

_____

6. The bears come home.

_____

7. The bears find Goldilocks asleep.

_____

8. They chase Goldilocks away.

_____

Name _____

- An **abbreviation** is a short form of a word.
- Most titles of people are abbreviations.
- An abbreviation begins with a capital letter and ends with a period.

Mister Fox
3 Forest Street
Portland, Oregon 97204

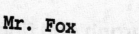

Mr. Fox
3 Forest St.
Portland, Oregon 97204

Draw lines to match the words in the left column with the abbreviations in the right column.

1. Mister		Mrs.
2. Senior		Ave.
3. Doctor		Mr.
4. Avenue		St.
5. Captain		Sr.
6. Missus		Dr.
7. Street		Jr.
8. Junior		Capt.

Name _____

- An abbreviation is a short way of writing a word. It starts with a capital letter and ends with a period.

- Use an apostrophe and **-s** to make a singular noun possessive.

Read the paragraph and find the mistakes in abbreviations and possessive nouns. Rewrite the passage correctly on the lines below.

   dr. Chen is a childrens doctor. He has lots of book's in the waiting room. mrs Gomez, the nurse, enjoys reading to the children when she has time. "mr Poppleton" is everyones' favorite story.

_____

_____

_____

_____

Name _____

Write the underlined word that is an action verb.

1. **Pedro** **makes** up great **stories**. _____

2. In one story, a **giant** ape **eats** a **huge** forest. _____

3. The ape **swallows** **whole** trees in **one** gulp. _____

4. Other **animals** **live** in the **trees**. _____

5. They **lose** their **homes** **because** of the ape. _____

6. So **they** **move** to the big **city**. _____

7. The animals **find** **new** homes in the city **parks**. _____

8. The giant **ape** **misses** the **other** animals. _____

9. **He** **plants** lots and lots of **new** trees. _____

10. **Soon** the animals **return** to the **forest**. _____

Name _____

- The tense of a verb tells when the action takes place.
- Present-tense verbs tell about actions that happen now.

  Josh <u>plays</u> ice hockey.

  His mom <u>watches</u> every game.

Draw a line under each present-tense verb. Then write the verb on the line.

1. Josh puts on his hockey skates. _____

2. He wears a helmet on his head. _____

3. Pads protect his knees. _____

4. Josh skates fast. _____

5. He slaps the puck with a hockey stick. _____

6. Josh's mom cheers for him. _____

- A present-tense verb must agree with its subject.
- Add **-s** to most verbs if the subject is singular. Add **-es** to verbs that end with **s**, **ch**, **sh**, **x**, or **z**.

   The car <u>stops</u> for the red light.

- Do not add **-s** or **-es** if the subject is plural.

   The children <u>cross</u> the street.

Draw a line under the correct present-tense verb in ( ). Then write another sentence using the same verb on the line below.

1. The woman (push, pushes) the swing gently.

   _____

2. The child (giggles, giggle).

   _____

3. The children (goes, go) down the slide one at a time.

   _____

4. Two boys (ride, rides) their bikes around the park.

   _____

5. One boy (wear, wears) a red helmet to stay safe.

   _____

6. The other (have, has) a green helmet on his head.

   _____

- Use commas to separate three or more words in a series.
- Use **and** or **or** before the last word in a series.

  We play sports in summer, winter, spring, <u>and</u> fall.

Find the missing commas and rewrite each sentence correctly on the lines below.

1. We go skiing skating and sledding during the winter.

_____

_____

2. I ski slowly carefully and safely.

_____

_____

3. Do you like to ice skate roller skate or rollerblade?

_____

_____

4. I wear a helmet knee pads and elbow pads when I skate.

_____

_____

5. We can go sledding in my yard at the school or in the park.

_____

_____

- A present-tense verb must agree with its subject.

- Add **-s** or **-es** if the verb is singular.

- Use commas to separate three or more words
  in a series.

**Find mistakes in the paragraph. Then rewrite the
paragraph correctly on the lines below.**

Each year a firefighter police officer or emergency
worker come to our school. The firefighter teach us about
stop drop and roll. The police officer tell us not to talks
to strangers. We learns about 911 and giving our name
number and address in an emergency.

_____

_____

_____

_____

_____

_____

Name _____

**Write the present tense of the verb in ( ) to complete
each sentence.**

1. Rose _____ for the light to change. (watch)

2. Her little sisters _____ Mom's hands. (hold)

3. They all _____ both ways before crossing. (look)

4. Rose _____ about safety at school and at home.
   (learn)

5. The students in Rose's class _____ posters. (make)

6. Chan _____ a list of safety rules on his poster.
   (write)

7. One girl _____ a cartoon. (draw)

8. The cartoon _____ kids on skateboards. (show)

9. One skateboarder _____ too fast. (go)

10. The other skateboarders _____ safety rules.
    (follow)

© Macmillan/McGraw-Hill

Name _____

> • Verbs can tell about actions that already happened.
>
> • These verbs are in the **past tense**.
>
> • Add **-ed** to most verbs to tell about an action in the past.
>
>   Our class <u>learned</u> about fossils last week.
>
>   Our class <u>looked</u> at dinosaurs yesterday.

Circle the past-tense verb in each sentence. Write it on the line.

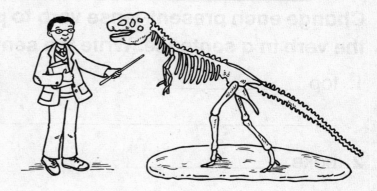

1. Our class visited the museum. _____

2. We learned about dinosaurs. _____

3. Did you know that dinosaurs once roamed the Earth?

   _____

4. I asked a question about Triceratops. _____

5. A scientist answered my question. _____

Choose one past-tense verb you circled above. Use it in a new sentence. Write the sentence on the lines.

6. _____

_____

Name _____

- If a verb ends with one consonant, double the consonant and add **-ed**.

  The car <u>stopped</u> at the red light.

- If a verb ends with **e**, drop the **e** and add **-ed**.

  The car <u>moved</u> at the green light.

Change each present-tense verb to past tense. Then use the verb in a sentence. Write the sentence on the line.

1. tap _____

   _____

2. bake _____

   _____

3. smile _____

   _____

4. trim _____

   _____

5. love _____

   _____

© Macmillan/McGraw-Hill

- Begin the greeting and closing in a letter with a capital letter.
- Use a comma after the greeting of a letter.
- Use a comma after the closing of a letter.

Find the mistakes in the letter. Rewrite the letter correctly on the lines below.

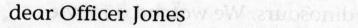

dear Officer Jones

Thank you for visiting our classroom.
We posted your safety tips on the wall. Stay safe.

yours truly,

Ms. Berger's class

_____

_____

_____

_____

_____

_____

- Add **-ed** to most verbs to tell about an action in the past.
- If a verb ends with one consonant, double the consonant and add **-ed**.
- If a verb ends with **e**, drop the **e** and add **-ed**.

Find the mistakes in the letter. Rewrite it correctly below.

dear Emily

Our teacher planed an awesome trip to the museum. We learnned all about dinosaurs. We watchd a movie about Tyrannosaurus Rex. We were most surprissed to see real dinosaur fossils.

your friend

Carlos

_____

_____

_____

_____

_____

Rewrite each sentence to tell about the past.
Change the underlined verb to the past tense.

I. The men and women <u>work</u> as a team.

_____

2. They <u>hunt</u> for dinosaur bones in the desert sand.

_____

3. One man <u>rams</u> his shovel into something hard.

_____

4. He <u>waves</u> to the other members of his team.

_____

5. Two women carefully <u>pick</u> up the dinosaur bones.

_____

6. They <u>ship</u> the bones home in a crate.

_____

7. Later, scientists <u>examine</u> the bones closely.

_____

8. They <u>learn</u> the size and shape of the dinosaur.

_____

- The verb **have** has a special form in the present tense.
- Use **has** when the subject is singular.

  Pete <u>has</u> tap shoes.

- Use **have** when the subject is plural or **I** or **you**.

  Marta and Joe <u>have</u> top hats.

  I <u>have</u> a cane.

A. Complete each sentence with *has* or *have*.

1. We _____ a school play in the winter.

2. My brother _____ a singing part.

3. My friends Lily and Sam _____ speaking parts.

4. I _____ a flute that I play in the band.

5. My teacher _____ a clarinet.

6. We all _____ a great time putting on the play.

B. Write one sentence with *has*. Write another sentence with *have*. Write them on the lines below.

7. _____

   _____

8. _____

   _____

© Macmillan/McGraw-Hill

Name _____

- The past-tense form of **have** is **had**.
- Use **had** in the past tense with any subject.

I <u>had</u> a dance recital.

My friends <u>had</u> fun watching me dance.

Change the verb *have* from present tense to past tense in each sentence. Write the new sentence on the lines.

1. We have our dance show in January.

_____

2. The show has three parts.

_____

3. I have a lead role.

_____

4. Juanita has a solo.

_____

5. We have a party after the show.

_____

Name _____

- Begin the first word and each important word in a book title with a capital letter.
- Underline the title of a book.

<u>A Very Young Dancer</u>

<u>Olivia Saves the Circus</u>

Correct the underlined book title in each sentence. Write it correctly on the line below.

1. <u>chasing vermeer</u> is a book about a famous artist.

_____

2. I just finished reading a book called <u>polly and the piano</u>.

_____

3. <u>the little ballerina</u> is my sister's favorite picture book.

_____

4. We read <u>the kids' guide to acting and stagecraft</u> to prepare for our school play.

_____

5. The library has a funny book called <u>angelina, star of the show</u>.

_____

- Use **has** in the present tense when the subject is singular. Use **have** when the subject is plural or **I** or **you**.

- The past-tense form of **have** is **had**.

- Capitalize the first letter and each important word in a book title.

Circle the mistakes in the sentences. Write the sentences correctly on the lines.

1. Our class is making a play of the book charlie and the chocolate factory.

_____

_____

2. We have tryouts yesterday.

_____

3. Alison have a great singing voice.

_____

4. Three boys has the part of Charlie.

_____

5. You has to come see our show!

_____

Circle the correct form of the verb *have* to complete each sentence.

1. My best friend Kim and I (have, has) big dreams.

2. Kim (have, has) dreams of being a singer on Broadway.

3. Even as a baby, she (has, had) a good voice.

4. Her dreams (have, has) a good chance of coming true.

5. Today, I (have, had) a dream of playing in a rock band.

6. My father (have, has) his old guitar in the garage.

7. He and his pals (have, had) a rock band a long time ago.

8. One of his friends (have, has) a music studio in the city.

9. Last week, I (have, had) my first lesson there.

10. I (have, has) a lot to learn before my first show.

- If two sentences have words that are the same, you can combine them.
- You can combine sentences by joining words with **and**.

The horses eat hay.   The horses play in the field.

The horses eat hay and play in the field.

**Combine each pair of sentences by using the word *and*.
Write the new sentence on the line.**

I. **a.** The cows live in the barn.
   b. The horses live in the barn.

   _____

   _____

2. **a.** Farmer Brown wakes up early.
   b. Farmer Brown goes to bed early.

   _____

   _____

3. **a.** Mrs. Brown plants corn.
   b. Mrs. Brown eats corn.

   _____

   _____

4. **a.** The children milk the cows.
   b. The children feed the chickens.

   _____

   _____

- If sentences have subjects that are the same, you can **combine** them.
- Sometimes you can combine sentences by joining two predicates with **and**.

  The cow slept.   The cow ate.

  The cow slept and ate.

Combine each pair of sentences by joining the predicates with the word *and*. Write the new sentences on the lines.

I. **a.** The cows walk in the field.
   b. The cows eat grass.

   _____

2. **a.** The farmer sits on a stool.
   b. The farmer milks the cow.

   _____

3. **a.** The pigs roll in the mud.
   b. The pigs get dirty.

   _____

4. **a.** The barn is big.
   b. The barn has red sides.

   _____

- End statements and commands with a period.
- End a question with a question mark.
- End an exclamation with an exclamation point.

Who will feed the pigs?   Sarah will feed the pigs.

Feed the pigs now.   Oh no, I spilled the food!

Read each sentence and add the correct punctuation.

1. Did you hear the rooster _____

2. Wake up and get dressed _____

3. I'm so tired _____

4. What's for breakfast _____

5. Please feed the chickens _____

6. I like to feed the animals _____

7. Which animal do you like best _____

8. The piglets are so cute _____

9. Who will clean the chicken coop _____

10. The chicken coop is a mess _____

- Sometimes you can **combine sentences** by joining two predicates with **and**.

- End a statement or a command with a period.

- End a question with a question mark.

- End an exclamation with an exclamation point.

Rewrite the paragraph correctly on the lines below. Add punctuation and combine sentences with the same subjects.

Have you ever been to a farm Our class went on a trip to a farm. Our class saw lots of animals. We watched baby chicks hop around We watched pigs play in the mud Boy, did those pigs get dirty

_____

_____

_____

_____

Circle the parts of the sentences that can be combined with the word *and*. Combine the sentences. Write the new sentence on the line.

1. Most farmers get up before dawn.

Most farmers work until sunset.

_____

_____

2. Farm children do chores before school.

Farm children do chores after school.

_____

_____

3. Beans grow in the field.

Tomatoes grow in the field.

_____

_____

4. The crops need water to grow.

The crops need sunlight to grow.

_____

_____

5. People stop at the farm stand.

People buy freshly picked corn.

_____

_____

Name _____

- A **linking verb** is a verb that does not show action.
- The verb **be** is a linking verb.
- The verb **be** has special forms in the present tense (**is, are, am**).

    The panda bear <u>is</u> cute.   Pelicans <u>are</u> birds.

    I <u>am</u> at the zoo.

Write *am, is,* or *are* to complete each sentence.

1. Mammals _____ warm-blooded.

2. A cow _____ a mammal.

3. Dolphins _____ mammals, too.

4. I _____ a mammal!

5. Cows _____ plant eaters.

6. A dolphin _____ a meat eater.

7. I _____ a meat eater, too.

8. What _____ your favorite kind of mammal?

- The past-tense form for **am** is **was**.
- The past-tense form for **is** is **was**.
- The past-tense form for **are** is **were**.

I <u>am</u> at the park. Yesterday, I <u>was</u> at the farm.

The chick <u>is</u> in the yard. Earlier, it <u>was</u> in the barn.

The bears <u>are</u> sleepy. In the spring, they <u>were</u> active.

Choose the correct linking verb in ( ). Then write the complete sentence below.

1. Yesterday I (was, were) in the woods.

_____

2. There (was, were) a deer eating leaves.

_____

3. The birds (was, were) in the air.

_____

4. A squirrel (was, were) up in a tree.

_____

5. It (was, were) very peaceful.

_____

- A proper noun begins with a capital letter.
- The name of a day, month, or holiday begins with a capital letter.

My dog Ralph had puppies in June.

Find capitalization mistakes in the sentences. Write the corrected sentences on the lines below.

I. memorial day was last monday.

_____

2. molly jones went fishing with her family.

_____

3. The month of may is a nice time to go fishing.

_____

4. Molly's brother ted caught a bass.

_____

5. Mr. jones fried the fish for lunch on tuesday.

_____

Name _____

- The words *is*, *are*, *am*, *was*, and *were* can be **linking verbs**.

Read the paragraph and find the mistakes. Rewrite the passage correctly on the lines below.

Brown bears is one of the largest types of bears. A female brown bear are about half the size of a male. These bears has thick fur that are usually brown. Some bears is lighter, and others is almost black. Brown bear cubs are born between january and march.

_____

_____

_____

_____

_____

_____

Name _____

Circle the present form of the verb *be* in each sentence. Rewrite the sentence. Change the verb to past tense.

1. I am at the kitchen window.

_____

2. The leaves of the maple tree are bright red.

_____

3. A chipmunk is in the grass.

_____

4. Its nest is under the ground.

_____

5. Some nuts and seeds are on the grass.

_____

6. The chipmunk's cheeks are full.

_____

- A **helping verb** helps another verb show an action.
- *Have* and *has* can be helping verbs.

  The bear <u>has</u> found berries.

  The birds <u>have</u> built a nest.

Write *has* or *have* to complete each sentence.

1. The mother bird _____ been searching for food.

2. She _____ found worms for her chicks.

3. The chicks _____ eaten the worms.

4. Oh no, the nest _____ fallen out of the tree!

5. Some foxes _____ spotted the nest.

6. I hope those foxes _____ already had their lunch!

7. The mother bird _____ tried to protect her chicks.

8. The chicks _____ escaped!

Name _____

- A **helping verb** helps another verb show an action.
- *Is, are, am, was,* and *were* can be helping verbs.

  A fox <u>is</u> looking for food.

  The bears <u>are</u> hibernating.

  I <u>am</u> watching the birds fly south.

  The squirrels <u>were</u> gathering nuts.

**Choose the correct helping verb in ( ).
Then write the complete sentence
below.**

1. The chicks (was, were) following their mother.

   _____

2. The mother bird (was, were) protecting her babies.

   _____

3. One chick (is, are) pecking around for food.

   _____

4. Another chick (is, are) hiding behind its mother.

   _____

5. I (am, are) watching the chicks.

   _____

Name _____

- Quotation marks set off the exact words of a person.
- Use quotation marks at the beginning and end of what a person says.
  "Do you see the rabbit?" asked Noah.

Find the mistakes in the sentences. Write the corrected sentences on the lines below.

1. I see a rabbit, said Ben.

_____

2. Noah said, It's so fast!

_____

3. Where is it going? asked Kim.

_____

4. It's going into the garden, replied Noah.

_____

5. Ben asked Do you think it's hungry?

_____

6. Let's follow it! said Kim.

_____

Name _____

- *Have, has, is, are, am, was,* and *were* can be **helping verbs**.
- Use quotation marks at the beginning and end of what a person says.

Read the paragraph and find the mistakes. Rewrite the passage correctly on the lines below.

In school we is learning about gorillas. Gorillas are large and gentle apes said our teacher. We read that they live in africa. We has also learned that gorillas eat vegetables. I is excited to learn more about gorillas.

_____

_____

_____

_____

_____

_____

Name _____

Mark the correct helping verb to complete each sentence.

1. The whales _____ been searching for food.

    ○ have   ○ has

    ○ is   ○ are

2. People _____ fishing in the same part of the sea.

    ○ has   ○ am

    ○ have   ○ are

3. A fishing line _____ become stuck in a whale's jaw.

    ○ is   ○ has

    ○ were   ○ am

4. The whale can't eat and _____ getting weak.

    ○ have   ○ am

    ○ is   ○ are

5. People _____ working hard to help the whale.

    ○ were   ○ have

    ○ has   ○ is

6. They _____ untangled the line and saved the whale.

    ○ has   ○ am

    ○ are   ○ have

- Some verbs do not add *-ed* to form the past tense.
- The verbs *go* and *do* have special forms in the past tense.

| I, we, you, they | go | went |
| I, we, you, they | do | did |

Choose the correct verb in ( ). Then write the complete sentence below.

I. Our class (go, went) to the library to learn about pollution.

_____

_____

2. We can (do, did) a lot to stop pollution.

_____

3. Toxic wastes should not (go, went) into the ocean.

_____

4. What are you going to (do, did) to stop pollution?

_____

5. Last summer we (go, went) to clean-up day at the beach.

_____

_____

6. Everyone (do, did) a lot of work picking up trash.

_____

- The verbs **_say_** and **_see_** have special forms in the past tense.

| I, we, you, they | see | saw |
| I, we, you, they | say | said |

Rewrite the sentences using the past tense of the verb in dark type.

1. I **see** a boy litter.

_____

2. I **say,** "Don't pollute!"

_____

3. We **see** him pick up his garbage.

_____

4. "Thank you!" we **say**.

_____

5. The children **see** lots of people litter.

_____

6. "Clean up!" the children **say** to all of them.

_____

- Begin the first word and each important word in a book title with a capital letter.
- Underline all the words in the title of a book.

  <u>Flash, Crash, Rumble, and Roll</u>

  <u>Feel the Wind</u>

Correct the underlined book title in each sentence. Write the title correctly on the line below.

1. I read **the kids' book of weather forecasting** to learn about weather.

   _____

2. **feel the wind** is a book about what causes wind.

   _____

3. The book **rain tonight** is about a real hurricane.

   _____

4. Charlie loves the book **night of the twisters** by Ivy Ruckman.

   _____

5. To learn about volcanoes, read **forces of nature**.

   _____

- The verbs **come**, **run**, **give**, and **sing** have special forms in the past tense.
- Begin the first word and each important word in a book title with a capital letter.
- Underline all the words in the title of a book.

Read the paragraph and find the mistakes. Rewrite the passage correctly on the lines below.

Only two friends comed to my party because of the blizzard. We runned around in the snow and had fun. One friend give me a book called blizzards and ice storms. What a perfect present, I said. Then they singed Happy Birthday to me, and we ate cake.

_____

_____

_____

_____

_____

_____

Name _____

Write the past tense of the verb in ( ) to complete each sentence.

1. I _____ a movie about helping our planet. (see)

2. Our teacher _____ we have to change bad habits. (say)

3. Mark, _____ you see the dripping faucet? (do)

4. The water _____ down the drain and was wasted. (go)

5. Mom _____ that the TV was on, but we weren't there. (see)

6. All the children _____ to bed. (go)

7. They _____ they forgot to turn off the TV. (say)

8. In the past, we _____ many things without thinking. (do)

Name _____

- Some verbs do not add **-ed** to form the past tense.
- The verbs **come** and **run** have special forms in the past tense.

I, we, you, they	come	came
I, we, you, they	run	ran

Circle the correct verb in ( ) to complete each sentence.

1. Mark (comed, came) home when the storm began.

2. The rain (comed, came) down fast and hard.

3. I (ran, runned) home quickly, too.

4. On his way, Mark (ran, runned) into a store.

5. Emily and Tia (come, came) into the store, too.

6. Together they (runned, ran) through the raindrops.

7. When they (came, come) inside, they were soaking wet.

8. Mark and I (runned, ran) to get towels.

Name _____

- Some verbs do not add **-ed** to form the past tense.
- The verbs **give** and **sing** have special forms in the past tense.

| I, we, you, they | give | gave |
| I, we, you, they | sing | sang |

Change the words in dark type to past tense. Write the new sentences on the lines below.

1. I **sing** the song about raindrops.

   _____

2. I **give** my old snow boots to my little brother.

   _____

3. We **sing** in a high voice.

   _____

4. They **sing** in a low voice.

   _____

5. We **give** our winter coats to charity.

   _____

6. You **give** money for hurricane victims, too.

   _____

- Capitalize the greeting and closing in a letter.
- Use a comma after the greeting and closing in a letter.
- Use a comma between the day and the year in a date.
- Use a comma between the names of a city and a state.

Find the mistakes in the letter. Write the corrected letter on the lines below.

42 Elm Road
Atlanta Georgia
May 9 2007

dear Rachel

We are going to Hawaii on june 6 2007. We will visit a rain forest. Do you want to go with us?

your pal
Elena

_____

_____

_____

_____

_____

_____

Name _____

- The verbs **come**, **run**, **give**, and **sing** have special forms in the past tense.
- The first word and each important word in a book title begin with a capital letter.
- Underline all the words in the title of a book.

Read the paragraph and find the mistakes. Rewrite the passage correctly on the lines below.

Only two friends comed to my party because of the blizzard. We runned around in the snow and had fun. One friend give me a book called blizzards and ice storms. What a perfect present, I said. Then they singed Happy Birthday to me, and we ate cake.

_____

_____

_____

_____

_____

_____

Make a check [✓] next to a sentence if the underlined past-tense verb is correct. Make an X if the verb is not correct.

1. This morning we <u>singed</u> a song about the weather.

2. Then Matt and Meytal <u>gave</u> the daily weather report.

3. The heavy rain that <u>came</u> in overnight will stop by noon.

4. That <u>gived</u> us a chance to go outside.

5. After lunch we <u>runned</u> around in the schoolyard.

6. A small yellow bird <u>sang</u> sweetly from a tree.

7. The sun <u>comed</u> out from behind the clouds.

8. Paul <u>ran</u> and jumped over the large puddles.

Rewrite the sentences you marked X correctly on the lines.

_____

_____

_____

_____

Name _____

- A **contraction** is a short form of two words.
- An **apostrophe** (') takes the place of the letters that are left out.

| is not | isn't | are not | aren't |
| has not | hasn't | have not | haven't |

Replace the underlined words with contractions. Write the new sentences on the lines.

1. The Arctic <u>is</u> <u>not</u> at the South Pole.

_____

2. The Arctic <u>is</u> <u>not</u> warm.

_____

3. There <u>are</u> <u>not</u> any trees in the Arctic.

_____

4. I <u>have</u> <u>not</u> been to the Arctic.

_____

5. Glen <u>has</u> <u>not</u> been there either.

_____

6. <u>Are</u> you <u>not</u> going to the Arctic next summer?

_____

Name _____

- A **contraction** is a short form of two words.
- An **apostrophe** (') takes the place of the letters that are left out.
- ***Doesn't***, ***don't***, ***didn't***, and ***can't*** are contractions.

does not = <u>doesn't</u>   do not = <u>don't</u>

did not = <u>didn't</u>   can not = <u>can't</u>

Replace the underlined words with contractions. Write the new sentences on the lines.

I. Many animals <u>can not</u> live in the Arctic.

_____

2. They <u>do not</u> do well in the cold weather.

_____

3. Most birds <u>can not</u> live in the Arctic all year.

_____

4. The tern <u>does not</u> stay for the winter.

_____

5. <u>Do not</u> be afraid of the Arctic wolf.

_____

6. The Arctic hare <u>did not</u> see the wolf.

_____

Name _____

- A **contraction** is a short form of two words.
- An **apostrophe** (') takes the place of the letters that are left out.

**Add the apostrophe to each contraction. Write the
contraction correctly on the line.**

I. Living in the Arctic isnt easy. _____

2. Most animals arent adapted to life in the Arctic. _____

3. Arctic wolf pups cant see or hear. _____

4. The cold doesnt get through the polar bear's thick fur.

_____

5. Some Arctic animals arent easy to see in the snow.

_____

6. Arctic hares dont want to run into a wolf. _____

7. The musk ox isnt friendly with the wolf. _____

8. We didnt see the walrus come out of the water. _____

- A **contraction** is a short form of two words.
- An **apostrophe** (') takes the place of the letters that are left out of a contraction.

Read the paragraph and find the contraction and book punctuation mistakes. Rewrite the paragraph correctly on the lines below.

In the book the lives of arctic animals, I read that Arctic animals dont get cold. It isnt' just a book about animals. I also learned that the sun does'nt come out in the winter at the North Pole. Did you know that there ar'ent any trees in the Arctic?

_____

_____

_____

_____

_____

Underline two words in each sentence that could be used to form a contraction. Then write the contractions on the lines below.

1. Some animals do not stay awake in cold weather.

2. The bears have not been awake for most of the winter.

3. A bear's heartbeat is not as fast while it sleeps.

4. There are not a lot of things for bears to eat in winter.

5. The bear does not need to eat during this time.

6. It has not used up all the energy stored in its body fat.

7. Other animals can not go so long without food.

8. I did not know that snakes and frogs sleep in winter.

1. _____   2. _____

3. _____   4. _____

5. _____   6. _____

7. _____   8. _____

Name _____

- A **pronoun** is a word that takes the place of a noun or nouns.
- A pronoun must agree with the noun it replaces.
- The pronouns **I, he, she, it,** and **you** can take the place of a singular noun.

  She touched the desert sand.   It was very hot.
  Do you know where the desert is?   I know where it is.
  He knows where the desert is, too.

Circle a pronoun to replace the underlined noun in each sentence.

1. Mina went on a trip to the Mojave Desert.   She   It

2. The desert was hot and dry.   He   It

3. Mina's brother saw a cactus.   He   It

4. The cactus was green and prickly.   He   It

5. Mina saw a Gila Monster!   She   He

6. Did you know that a Gila Monster is a lizard?   she   it

7. Mina was scared!   It   She

8. Mina's dad was a little scared, too.   He   She

Name _____

- A plural noun names more than one person, place, or thing.
- The **pronouns** *we*, *you*, and *they* can take the place of a plural noun or more than one noun or pronoun.

<u>Rattlesnakes</u> are dangerous.   <u>They</u> are dangerous.
<u>Emma and I</u> saw a rattlesnake.   <u>We</u> saw a rattlesnake.

Circle the correct pronoun in ( ) to complete each sentence.

1. Jamal and Nora are going to catch the snakes. We're glad (you, she) are here, Jamal and Nora!

2. Now (we, I) are safe!

3. Did you hear the wolves? (We, They) are howling.

4. Wolves don't eat people, so (we, she) are not in danger.

5. Mom and I hope to see wolf pups. (They, He) are so cute!

6. Have (you, she) ever seen a wolf pup?

7. How big does (it, they) grow?

8. (I, We) are having so much fun in the desert.

© Macmillan/McGraw-Hill

Name _____

- **Quotation marks** set off the exact words of a speaker.
- Use quotation marks (" ") at the beginning and end of what a person says.

  "How hot is the desert?" asked Lydia.

Read the sentences. Write the sentences correctly on the lines.

1. Where is the Sahara Desert? asked Maria.

   _____

2. It is in Africa, said Ms. Jackson.

   _____

3. The Sahara is the largest desert! said our teacher.

   _____

4. How big is the Sahara Desert? asked Jared.

   _____

5. It covers 35,000,000 miles! said Ms. Jackson.

   _____

6. Which desert is the smallest? Ms. Jackson asked.

   _____

7. Where is the smallest desert? asked James.

   _____

8. It's in Canada, said Ms. Jackson.

   _____

• A **pronoun** must agree with the noun it replaces.

Find each mistake. Then rewrite the paragraphs correctly on the lines below.

Mr. Walker taught the class what him knows about desert plants. She said, The desert is home to many plants. How can they grow in dry deserts? he asked.

Some desert plants store water in their roots, said Leah.

She are right! said Mr. Walker.

_____

_____

_____

_____

_____

_____

© Macmillan/McGraw-Hill

Name _____

Mark the pronoun that could replace the underlined words.

1. <u>Ruby</u> is in the first car with Dad and Seth.

   ○ They   ○ She   ○ I   ○ We

2. <u>Mom and the two younger boys</u> were in the other car.

   ○ I   ○ They   ○ It   ○ He

3. <u>Mr. Ali</u> will be our guide through the desert.

   ○ She   ○ They   ○ He   ○ It

4. <u>Anna</u> was surprised to see so many flowers and plants.

   ○ I   ○ They   ○ It   ○ He

5. "<u>The desert</u> is not a dead place," Mr. Ali said.

   ○ You   ○ It   ○ He   ○ We

6. <u>Ruby and I</u> took pictures of the giant cactus.

   ○ We   ○ She   ○ It   ○ He

7. <u>The giant cactus</u> had branches that looked like arms.

   ○ You   ○ We   ○ It   ○ They

8. <u>Ruby and Anna</u> can eat the fruit of the giant cactus.

   ○ It   ○ She   ○ I   ○ You

Name _____

- Use **I** in the subject part of the sentence.

- Use **me** in the predicate part of the sentence.

- Name yourself last when talking about yourself and another person.

  <u>I</u> have a dancing part in the show.

  The teacher helps <u>me</u> learn the steps.

Write *I* or *me* to complete each sentence.

1. Isabel and _____ are trying out for a play.

2. The director calls _____ in first.

3. Isabel wishes _____ luck.

4. _____ am so nervous!

5. The director asks _____ to read from a script.

6. After I read, he thanks _____.

7. Next he asks _____ to sing a song.

8. Isabel and _____ hope we get parts in the play.

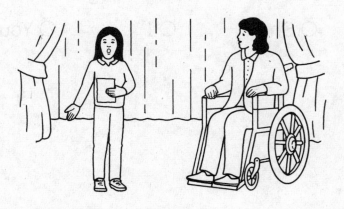

- Use **we** and **us** when you talk about yourself and another person.
- Use **we** in the subject part of the sentence.
- Use **us** in the predicate part.

    We will wear tutus in the dance show.

    Mom will help us make our costumes.

**Replace the underlined words with
we or *us*. Write the new sentence
on the line below.**

1. Jackie and I love to dance!

_____

2. Our teacher asked Jackie and me to dance in the school play.

_____

3. Jackie and I will learn all the steps.

_____

4. Jackie and I will practice every day.

_____

5. The audience will like Jackie and me.

_____

6. They will throw roses at Jackie and me.

_____

Name _____

> - The pronoun **I** is always a capital letter.
> - Use **I** in the subject of a sentence.

Correct the sentences and write them on the lines.

I. i was the king in the school play.

_____

2. Mara and i sang a song together.

_____

3. i had many lines to learn.

_____

4. The queen and i danced together

_____

5. At the end of the play, i took a bow.

_____

6. Matt and i went for ice cream after the play.

_____

- Use **I** and **we** in the subject of a sentence.
- Use **me** and **us** in the predicate part of a sentence.
- The pronoun **I** is always a capital letter.
- Name yourself last when talking about yourself and another person.

Circle each mistake in the use of pronouns. Then rewrite the paragraph correctly on the lines below.

Mom and me went to see a musical. The usher gave i a program and showed we where to sit. Us had great seats! i could see the actors right up close. i hope Mom takes I to another show soon!

_____

_____

_____

_____

_____

Name _____

Write C if the underlined pronoun is correct. If the pronoun is not correct, cross it out and write the correct pronoun on the line.

1. What play do you think <u>us</u> should put on? _____

2. <u>I</u> would like to write a new play. _____

3. Henry and <u>me</u> would like to help you. _____

4. They asked Hasheem and <u>I</u> to make the set. _____

5. Would you like <u>we</u> two to work on the costumes? _____

6. Tomorrow Ann and <u>me</u> will print the programs. _____

7. Can someone help Joe and <u>I</u> with our lines? _____

8. <u>We</u> can't wait until opening night. _____

9. The audience clapped a long time for <u>us</u>. _____

10. Next year the kids and <u>I</u> want to do a musical. _____

- A **possessive pronoun** takes the place of a possessive noun.

- A possessive pronoun shows who or what owns something.

- *My, your, his,* and *her* are possessive pronouns.

This is <u>my</u> globe.   This is <u>your</u> map.

Where is <u>his</u> house?   Here is <u>her</u> car.

Circle the correct possessive noun in ( ) for each sentence. Write it on the line.

1. (Me, My) favorite explorer is Christopher Columbus. _____

2. (His, He) ships were called the *Niña, Pinta,* and *Santa Maria.*
   _____

3. (Him, His) journey was very long. _____

4. I followed it on (my, me) map. _____

5. Sacajawea is (your, you) favorite explorer. _____

6. (She, Her) journey was very important in U.S. history.
   _____

7. Sacajawea tied (her, she) baby to her back. _____

8. Did you trace (her, she) journey on the map? _____

Name _____

- A **possessive pronoun** shows who or what owns something. Some possessive pronouns are *its, our, your,* and *their*.

  <u>Our</u> house is on Elm Street.   <u>Their</u> house is on Oak Street.

  <u>Your</u> house is pretty.   <u>Its</u> color is pink.

Underline the correct possessive nouns. Write the sentences correctly on the lines.

1. (Us, Our) class is learning about Alexander Graham Bell and Thomas Watson.

   _____

2. (Their, They) invention changed the way we live.

   _____

3. Can you imagine (your, our) life without a telephone?

   _____

4. (It's, Its) technology helps us to stay in touch.

   _____

5. What inventor will (our, its) teacher tell us about next?

   _____

6. What is (your, you're) favorite invention?

   _____

Name _____

- A proper noun begins with a capital letter.
- The name of a day, month, or holiday begins with a capital letter.

   <u>Columbus Day</u> is the second <u>Monday</u> in <u>October</u>.

Find the mistakes. Write the corrected sentences on the lines.

I. colorado was the first state to observe columbus day.

_____

_____

2. memorial day is the last monday in may.

_____

3. Both abraham lincoln and george washington were both born in february.

_____

_____

4. The third monday in february is presidents' day.

_____

_____

5. President truman declared june 14 flag day.

_____

6. I was born on sunday, august 17.

_____

- A **possessive pronoun** takes the place of a possessive noun.

- A possessive pronoun shows who or what owns something. Some possessive pronouns are *my, your, his, its, our, your,* and *their*.

- A proper noun begins with a capital letter.

- The name of a day, month, or holiday begins with a capital letter.

Find the mistakes. Rewrite the paragraph correctly on the lines below.

Me twin brothers have a birthday on presidents' day. There party is on saturday, february 18. Us parents got the boys a puppy as a present. Their name is gus. Gus will sleep in them room.

_____

_____

_____

_____

_____

_____

© Macmillan/McGraw-Hill

Name _____

Underline the possessive pronoun that completes each sentence correctly. Write it on the line.

1. "This is _____ new invention," said Sammy.

   my   me   I

2. "_____ invention is a very strange looking thing," Tito said.

   Your   Its   Our

3. "Where is _____ on and off switch?" Kayla asked.

   me   you   its

4. Kayla wanted to show off _____ own invention next.

   she   her   its

5. Sammy put _____ hand on the small black switch.

   his   you   me

6. "Should we all cover _____ eyes?" Ina asked.

   her   my   our

7. To be safe, the kids moved _____ chairs back.

   its   their   they

8. "Hold on to _____ hats, kids!" Sammy said with a grin.

   your   its   their

- A **contraction** is a short form of two words put together.
- An apostrophe (') takes the place of the letter or letters that are left out.
- Some contractions are formed by putting together pronouns and verbs.

  I am   I'm   she is   she's   he is   he's

A. Write the contraction for the underlined words in each sentence.

1. I am looking at the moon. _____

2. He is gazing at the stars. _____

3. She is an astronaut. _____

4. I am very interested in the moon. _____

5. He is going to teach me about the stars. _____

B. Write the two words that were put together to form each contraction.

6. She's flying to the moon. _____

7. He's going with her. _____

8. I'm going to fly to the moon one day. _____

© Macmillan/McGraw-Hill

Name _____

- A **contraction** is a short form of two words put together.

- An apostrophe (') takes the place of the missing letter or letters in the contraction.

| it is | <u>it's</u> | we are | <u>we're</u> |
| they are | <u>they're</u> | you are | <u>you're</u> |

Write the contraction for the underlined words.
Write the new sentence on the line below.

1. <u>It is</u> a starry night. _____

   _____

2. <u>We are</u> gazing at the stars. _____

   _____

3. <u>They are</u> beautiful! _____

   _____

4. <u>It is</u> going to be nice tomorrow. _____

   _____

5. <u>You are</u> reading books about stars. _____

   _____

Name _____

- Remember that an apostrophe takes the place of the letter or letters that are left out of a contraction.

- Possessive pronouns, such as **their, your,** and **its,** do not have apostrophes.

- Do not confuse possessive pronouns with contractions. Some of them sound the same, but are spelled differently and have different meanings.

Possessive Pronoun	Contraction
their	they're
your	you're
its	it's

Read each sentence. Write the correct pronoun or contraction on the line.

1. (They're, Their) teacher is teaching a lesson about the moon.

   _____

2. (Their, They're) reading the book Rocket to the Moon.

   _____

3. (Its, It's) about the first lunar landing. _____

4. Are they almost finished with (they're their) book? _____

5. (Your, You're) reading a book called The Moon. _____

6. What is (your, you're) book about? _____

7. The book is about the moon and (it's, its) phases. _____

8. (Its, It's) full of interesting facts. _____

Name _____

- An apostrophe (') takes the place of the letters left out of a contraction.

- Possessive pronouns do not have apostrophes.

- The present-tense verb must agree with a pronoun in the subject part of a sentence.

Rewrite the paragraph correctly on the lines.

Were learning about the moon. Mr. Jones know a lot about the moon. Hes an expert! He say the moon cannot be seen at the start of it's cycle. Its called the New Moon.

_____

_____

_____

_____

_____

_____

Name _____

Underline two words in each sentence that could be used to form a contraction. Then write the contractions on the lines below.

1. The book I am reading is about a family in the future.

2. It is a science fiction story.

3. In the story, they are living in a new colony on the moon.

4. The dad is an explorer, and he is on a space mission.

5. The mom is a scientist, but she is also in a rock band.

6. It sounds like you are enjoying the book.

7. Someday we are going to live on the moon.

8. Do you think it is really possible?

1. _____   2. _____

3. _____   4. _____

5. _____   6. _____

7. _____   8. _____

Name _____

- A present-tense verb must agree with a pronoun in the subject part of a sentence.
- With the pronouns **he, she,** and **it,** add **-s** to most verbs to form the present tense.

  <u>He picks</u> a flower.   <u>She smells</u> the rose.   <u>It smells</u> great.

Underline the verbs that agree with the pronouns. Write the sentences on the lines.

1. She (want, wants) to plant a garden.

_____

2. It (takes, take) hard work to plant a garden.

_____

3. She (buys, buy) seeds at the store.

_____

4. He (help, helps) her plant the seeds.

_____

5. He (waters, water) the garden.

_____

6. It (look, looks) good.

_____

- Remember that a present-tense verb must agree with its pronoun subject.

- With the pronouns *I, we, you,* and *they,* do **not** add *-s* to most action verbs to form the present tense.

  We visit your garden.   You show us around.

  I pick some tomatoes.   They taste great!

Circle the pronoun in ( ) that agrees with the verb in each sentence.

I. (You, She) enjoy gardening.

2. (We, He) think your garden is lovely.

3. What kind of flowers do (you, she) grow?

4. (I, He) see red roses.

5. (It, They) grow so tall!

6. How do (she, you) grow such pretty flowers?

7. (I, He) want to take some flowers home.

8. Can (we, us) pick the roses?

- Underline all the words in the title of a book.

- Begin the first word and each important word in a book title with a capital letter.

- Any unimportant word in a book title, such as **a, and, for, of, the,** and **to** should **not** begin with a capital letter unless it is the first word in the title.

<u>The Giant Carrot</u>   <u>The Big Book of Gardening</u>

Correct the book titles in the sentences. Write the titles correctly on the lines below.

1. In the book carlos and the squash plant, a squash grows out of a boy's ear!

_____

2. The book The Gardener won the Caldecott Honor Award.

_____

3. I read the book planting a rainbow to my little brother.

_____

4. From Seed to Plant is about how to grow a bean plant.

_____

5. How a seed grows tells how an acorn grows into an oak tree.

_____

- With the pronouns *he*, *she*, and *it*, add *-s* to most action verbs to form the present tense.

- With the pronouns *I*, *we*, *you*, and *they*, do **not** add *-s* to most action verbs to form the present tense.

- Begin the first word and all the important words in a book title with capital letters.

- Underline all the words in a book title.

Find the mistakes. Rewrite the paragraph correctly.

Mom and I goes to the library. She read <u>how to grow</u> <u>a garden</u>. I reads A Kid's Guide to Gardening. The books tells us how to grow a garden. We wants to plant flowers. We knows it take hard work.

_____

_____

_____

_____

_____

_____

Underline the pronoun subject in each sentence. Then rewrite the sentence. Make the present-tense verb agree with its pronoun subject.

1. We plants a garden in early spring.

_____

2. Do you thinks vegetables will grow well here?

_____

3. For a while, it seem that nothing happens.

_____

4. They waits patiently, and soon green shoots appear.

_____

5. One day I sees some white blossoms.

_____

6. Then he say, "Look, peppers are growing."

_____

7. They grows quickly under the warm sun.

_____

8. She pick peppers, peas, and lettuce.

_____

- An **adjective** is a word that describes a noun.
- Some adjectives tell what kind.

  <u>green</u> balloons   <u>big</u> balloons

Circle the adjective in each sentence. Underline the noun the adjective describes.

1. Luke is having a big party for his brother Paul.

2. He is making a chocolate cake.

3. He is putting vanilla frosting on top.

4. We are blowing up blue balloons.

5. I am hanging red streamers.

6. A funny clown will juggle at the party.

7. We got Paul a tricky puzzle for a present.

8. His parents got him new skates.

Name _____

- An **adjective** is a word that describes a noun.
- Some adjectives tell how many.

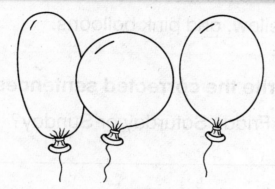

Circle the adjectives that tell how many. Then rewrite each sentence using a new amount.

1. My birthday is in three weeks.

   _____

2. I am inviting ten friends to my party.

   _____

3. Mom is blowing up a few balloons.

   _____

4. There will be nine candles on my cake.

   _____

5. One candle is for good luck.

   _____

6. There will be many sweet treats.

   _____

Name _____

> - Use commas to separate three or more items in a series.
> - Use **and** or **or** before the last word in a series.
>   I see green, yellow, and pink balloons.

Find the mistakes. Write the corrected sentences on the lines.

1. Is Kenda's party on Friday Saturday or Sunday?

_____

_____

2. We will listen to rock disco and jazz music.

_____

3. Kenda will wear a red white or yellow dress.

_____

4. Her mom made cupcakes brownies and cookies.

_____

5. Kenda filled goody bags with whistles stickers and bubbles.

_____

_____

6. Kenda's aunts uncles and cousins are coming to her party.

_____

_____

© Macmillan/McGraw-Hill

Name _____

- Use commas to separate three or more items in a series.

- An apostrophe takes the place of letters left out of a contraction.

- The present-tense verb must agree with a pronoun in the subject part of a sentence.

Find the mistakes. Rewrite the paragraph correctly on the lines.

Were throwing a surprise party for Maria Anna and Louisa. Their triplets! We'll serve sandwiches juice potato chips and chocolate cake. Were sure theyll be surprised.

_____

_____

_____

_____

_____

Name _____

Find the adjective and the noun it describes in each sentence. Write them on the lines.

1. Mom hangs colorful lanterns around the yard.

   adjective _____   noun _____

2. The full moon is shining in the sky.

   adjective _____   noun _____

3. We place the food on the four tables.

   adjective _____   noun _____

4. Yummy smells fill the air.

   adjective _____   noun _____

5. Three guests bring guitars.

   adjective _____   noun _____

6. They play some songs after we eat.

   adjective _____   noun _____

7. Grandma and Grandpa dance to their favorite tune.

   adjective _____   noun _____

8. Everyone says that it is a wonderful party.

   adjective _____   noun _____

- The words *a* and *an* are special adjectives called **articles**.
- Use the article *a* before a word that begins with a consonant sound.

    I read <u>a</u> book.   I write <u>a</u> story.

Write the correct article *a* or *an* on the line to complete each sentence.

1. Our teacher told us _____ story.

2. It is _____ fantasy story.

3. It was about _____ dog named Leo.

4. Leo liked to chase _____ cat named Lola.

5. One day Lola got stuck in _____ tree

6. _____ firefighter tried to get Lola out.

7. Our teacher wants us to come up with _____ ending.

8. I'm going to write _____ happy ending.

Name _____

> • The words *a* and *an* are special adjectives called articles.
> • Use the article *an* before a word that begins with a vowel sound.
>
>   I want to hear <u>an</u> animal tale.

Circle the correct article *a* or *an* to complete each sentence. Write the article on the line.

1. Have you heard the story about

    (a, an) ant named Azizi? _____

2. Azizi is (a, an) African name. _____

3. Azizi is (a, an) friendly ant. _____

4. He has (a, an) lot of friends. _____

5. One of Azizi's friends is (a, an) elephant. _____

6. He is also friendly with (a, an) kangaroo. _____

7. It is (a, an) interesting story. _____

8. What (a, an) great ending! _____

© Macmillan/McGraw-Hill

- Begin a proper noun with a capital letter.
- Begin an abbreviation of a person's title with a capital letter and end it with a period.

  <u>Mrs. Ortiz</u> read us a story.

Find mistakes in the sentences. Write the corrected sentences on the lines below.

1. mrs ortiz reads aloud a book by louis sachar.

_____

2. mr sachar won a newbery medal for the book <u>holes</u>.

_____

3. My favorite author is jon scieszka.

_____

4. I also like to read books by dr seuss.

_____

5. I hope mrs ortiz reads us a book by mr scieszka or dr seuss.

_____

Name _____

- Use the article **a** before a word that begins with a consonant sound.
- Use the article **an** before a word that begins with a vowel sound.
- Remember to capitalize proper nouns.
- Capitalize a person's title. If it is an abbreviation, end it with a period.

Find the mistakes. Rewrite the paragraph correctly on the lines.

ms campbell read us a story about a old lady who swallows an fly. She also swallows an bird, an goat, and even an horse! I think the old lady should have gone to see dr doolittle. He's a animal doctor!

_____

_____

_____

_____

_____

Name _____

Write *a* or *an* to complete each sentence correctly.

1. I have _____ aunt who writes children's books.

2. She wrote _____ book called <u>The Lion and the</u>
   <u>Mouse</u>.

3. In the story the lion gets trapped in _____ rope net.

4. The lion lets out _____ angry howl.

5. _____ little mouse hears the lion's cry.

6. "I have _____ idea," the mouse says. "I will help
   you."

7. "How could _____ animal as small you help me?"
   the lion asks.

8. The mouse shows the lion _____ mouthful of sharp
   teeth.

9. Then it begins to chew on _____ piece of rope.

10. Soon the net has _____ enormous hole in it, and the
    lion is set free.

Name _____

- **Synonyms** are words that have the same or almost the same meanings.
- Use synonyms to make your writing more interesting.

  stones/rocks   giant/big   friend/pal

Choose the synonym from the box for each underlined word. Write it on the line.

| like | pals | globe | wish | mail | hobby |

1. Emily has a penpal named Tahira on the other side of the world. _____

2. They <u>send</u> letters to each other every week. _____

3. Both girls <u>enjoy</u> writing. _____

4. Drawing is another favorite <u>activity</u>. _____

5. Emily and Tahira <u>hope</u> to meet each other one day.

   _____

6. They're sure they will be great <u>friends</u>. _____

Name _____

- **Antonyms** are words with opposite meanings.
- Understanding antonyms can help you better understand word meanings.

  happy/sad   loud/quiet   large/small

Write an antonym for the underlined word. Choose a word from the box.

| small | slow | mean | huge | happy | few |

1. Our teacher read us a <u>sad</u> folk tale from China.

   _____

2. The tale is about a <u>tiny</u> frog named Ling. _____

3. Ling was a <u>fast</u> hopper. _____

4. Ling had <u>many</u> friends. _____

5. One of Ling's friends was a <u>large</u> mouse. _____

6. She was a very <u>friendly</u> mouse. _____

- Begin every sentence with a capital letter.
- End a statement or a command with a period.
- End a question with a question mark.
- End an exclamation with an exclamation mark.

Find the mistakes. Write sentences correctly on the lines.

1. what country are Abby's great grandparents from

_____

_____

2. they came all the way from Poland by boat

_____

_____

3. rahim's family is from Africa

_____

4. show me where Africa is on a map

_____

5. where is your family from

_____

Name _____

- Begin every sentence with a capital letter.
- End statements and commands with a period.
- End a question with a question mark.
- End an exclamation with an exclamation mark.
- A proper noun begins with a capital letter.

**Find the mistakes. Rewrite the paragraph correctly
on the lines.**

a new boy joined our class today
his name is oren. do you know where
Oren is from. he moved here all the
way from Israel? "Please welcome
Oren," said our teacher

_____

_____

_____

_____

_____

Name _____

Write S if the underlined words are synonyms.
Write A if the underlined words are antonyms.

1. The world is <u>huge</u>, yet sometimes it seems <u>small</u>. _____

2. <u>Children</u> in America are like <u>kids</u> everywhere. _____

3. We <u>like</u> to play, and we <u>enjoy</u> being with friends. _____

4. One <u>sport</u> that we all know is the <u>game</u> of soccer. _____

5. I like soccer because it's <u>fast</u>, but I like a <u>slow</u> game of baseball, too. _____

6. Do you think baseball is <u>harder</u> or <u>easier</u> than soccer? _____

7. My friend Sangeeta has <u>always</u> played soccer, but she has <u>never</u> played baseball. _____

8. My <u>entire</u> family was born in America, and her <u>whole</u> family was born in India. _____

Write a sentence. Use a synonym for _happy_.

9. _____

Write a sentence. Use an antonym for _noisy_.

10. _____

Name _____

> • You can use **adjectives to compare** people, places, or things.
>
> • Add **-er** to an adjective to compare two nouns.
>   Navy blue is <u>darker</u> than sky blue.

Underline the adjective that compares in each sentence. Write it on the line.

1. Orange is a warmer color than blue. _____

2. Green is a cooler color than red. _____

3. My painting is bigger than your painting. _____

4. Your painting is brighter than my painting. _____

5. Henry has a thicker paintbrush than Carlos. _____

6 Tess has thinner crayons than Jing. _____

7. Yael thinks painting is harder than drawing. _____

8. Art class is longer than music class. _____

- You can use **adjectives to compare** people, places, or things.
- Add **-est** to an adjective to compare more than two nouns.

    Cymbals are the <u>loudest</u> instruments of all.

Look at the pictures and read the sentence. Write an adjective that ends with -est on the line.

1. The harp is the _____ instrument.

2. The square is the _____ shape.

3. Hannah is the _____ jumper.

4. Evan is the _____ runner.

5. Jenny is the _____ child.

- Add an apostrophe and **-s** to make a singular noun possessive.
- Add an apostrophe to make most plural nouns possessive.

Look at the one <u>boy's</u> painting.
Look at the two <u>boys'</u> paintings.

Find the mistakes. Write sentences correctly on the lines.

1. The two artists paintings are colorful.

_____

2. The taller womans artwork shows a forest.

_____

3. The shorter painters artwork shows a garden.

_____

4. My three sisters favorite artwork is the garden painting.

_____

_____

5. My moms favorite artwork is the forest painting.

_____

_____

Name _____

- Add *-er* to an adjective to compare two nouns.
- Add *-est* to an adjective to compare more than two nouns.
- Add an apostrophe and *s* to make a singular noun possessive.
- Add an apostrophe to make most plural nouns possessive.

Underline the correct adjective to complete each sentence. Add an apostrophe to each possessive noun. Write the sentence correctly on the line.

1. Tims painting is the (bigger, biggest) of the five.

   _____

2. Is Mayas painting (smaller, smallest) than Enricos painting?

   _____

3. The three boys easels are the (neater, neatest) in the class.

   _____

4. The second-graders paintbrushes are (thicker, thickest) than the third-graders brushes.

   _____

   _____

5. The teachers paintbrush is the (thinner, thinnest).

   _____

Name _____

**Mark the adjective that completes each
sentence correctly.**

1. I had a _____ time than Irena had in pottery class.

   ○ hardest   ○ harder

2. Maybe it's because she has _____ fingers than I have.

   ○ longer   ○ long

3. The second pot I made was _____ than the first.

   ○ nicest   ○ nicer

4. Irena made the _____ pot of all.

   ○ prettiest   ○ pretty

5. She is the _____ potter in our class.

   ○ finest   ○ fine

6. Of all the pots, Sam's has the _____ shape.

   ○ odder   ○ oddest

7. His pot is _____ and more colorful than mine.

   ○ big   ○ bigger

8. I painted my pot with the _____ red paint in the box.

   ○ brightest   ○ brighter

- An **adverb** tells more about a verb.

- An adverb can tell how.
    The inventor worked <u>slowly</u>.

Circle the verb in each sentence. Then write the adverb on the line.

1. The scientist spoke clearly about her invention. _____

2. The audience listened carefully. _____

3. A volunteer pulled the lever gently. _____

4. The robot moved suddenly. _____

5. The crowd cheered loudly. _____

6. The robot bowed gracefully. _____

- An **adverb** tells more about a verb.
- An adverb can tell when or where.
    An inventor visited our class <u>yesterday</u>. (when)
    She sat <u>nearby</u>. (where)

Circle the adverb in each sentence. On the lines, write the word *when* if it tells when. Write *where* if it tells where.

I. Long ago, George Washington Carver invented many uses for

peanuts. _____

2. The peanuts grew outside. _____

3. Do you think Mr. Carver lived nearby? _____

4. Mr. Carver never sold his inventions. _____

5. Finally, Mr. Carver won a medal for his work. _____

6. Which of Mr. Carver's inventions do you use today?

_____

- The pronoun *I* is always a capital letter.
- A proper noun begins with a capital letter.

    <u>I</u> visited an invention museum in <u>Chicago</u>.

Find the mistakes in capitalization.
Write sentences correctly.

1. i read a book about thomas edison.

_____

2. i learned that he had a laboratory in new jersey.

_____

_____

3. My dad and i are going to the edison museum in ohio.

_____

_____

4. i think edison's greatest invention was the movie projector.

_____

_____

5. One day i hope to be a great inventor like thomas edison.

_____

_____

© Macmillan/McGraw-Hill

- The pronoun *I* is always a capital letter.
- A proper noun begins with a capital letter.
- Add an apostrophe and -*s* to make a singular noun possessive.

Find the mistakes. Rewrite the paragraph correctly on the lines.

garrett morgan was an inventor from cleveland who worked to make peoples lives safer. morgans invention of the traffic signal made traveling safer. morgans' gas mask also kept people safe. i hope to create a life-saving invention one day.

_____

_____

_____

_____

_____

_____

Name _____

Write the underlined word in each sentence that is an adverb.

1. <u>Today</u>, <u>blood</u> is kept in blood banks. _____

2. In the 1940s, <u>Charles Drew</u> discovered a <u>better</u> way to

   collect blood <u>safely</u>. _____

3. He also <u>found</u> a way to <u>store</u> blood <u>longer</u>. _____

4. People <u>didn't</u> know as much <u>about</u> blood <u>then</u>.

   _____

5. As a <u>boy</u>, Charles Drew lived <u>happily</u> with <u>his</u> family in

   Washington, D.C. _____

6. He <u>got</u> up <u>early</u> to sell <u>papers</u> on street corners.

   _____

7. His <u>neighborhood</u> <u>had</u> a pool <u>nearby</u>. _____

8. He <u>soon</u> became a <u>star</u> <u>swimmer</u>. _____

9. Charles Drew <u>went</u> <u>away</u> to <u>college</u>. _____

10. <u>Later</u>, he <u>became</u> a doctor <u>and</u> teacher. _____